TED TURNER
Cable Television Tycoon

Makers of the Media

TED TURNER
Cable Television Tycoon

Jeremy Byman

MORGAN
REYNOLDS
Incorporated

Greensboro

TED TURNER: *Cable Television Tycoon*

Copyright © 1998 by Jeremy Byman

Photo Credits:
AP/Wide World Photos, The McCallie School
Jane Greene, Brown University Archives, Judy Nye Hallisy

Library of Congress Cataloging-in-Publication Data
Byman, Jeremy, 1944-
  Ted Turner : cable television tycoon / Jeremy Byman. —1st ed.
      p. cm. — (Makers of the media)
  Includes bibliographical references and index.
  Summary: A biography of the multimillionaire media pioneer, creator of the Cable News
Network, champion yachtsman, and founder of environmental and humanitarian
organizations.
   ISBN 1-883846-25-0
      1. Ted Turner—Juvenile literature. 2. Television broadcasting of news—United
States—Biography—Juvenile literature. 3. Telecommunication—United States—
Biography—Juvenile literature. 4. Businessmen—United States—Biography—Juvenile
literature. [1. Turner, Ted. 2. Businessmen. 3. Television broadcasting of news.
4. Telecommunication]
I. Title II. Series.
PN4888. T4B96 1998
384.55'5'092—dc21
[B]

                                                              98-5379
                                                                CIP
                                                                 AC

Printed in the United States of America
First Edition

To my parents,
Leonard and Eleanor Byman,
who always sent me to the dictionary.

Contents

Ted Turner

Chapter One

His Father's Son

1991 was Ted Turner's year of miracles.

On the night of January 16, the world watched as three television correspondents for the Cable News Network (CNN) broadcast to the world live television pictures of the beginning of the Persian Gulf War. Explosions lighted the night sky as American and British planes flew over Baghdad, bombarding the capital of Iraq. Peter Arnett, Bernard Shaw and John Holliman, three CNN reporters, took cover under a table in their hotel room and reported from "here at ground zero, feeling the ground rumble, hearing the thunder."

Shaw, Arnett, and Holliman were in Baghdad that night because they decided to take a chance. Their boss, Ted Turner, agreed they could stay, though the other news organizations had ordered their reporters to leave because of the danger.

That night and throughout the days that followed CNN broadcast the fighting live. Millions of people around the world saw Scud missiles flying over Israel and Saudi Arabia. They watched as Peter Arnett interviewed American prisoners of war. Saddam Hussein, the dictator of Iraq, even watched CNN as the United Nations troops destroyed his army. Other networks and stations throughout the world showed CNN's coverage.

In August of 1991, CNN proved again how important it was on the world stage when it helped to end an attempt by Soviet plotters to seize power. When Boris Yeltsin climbed on a tank and rallied his countrymen against the coup attempted by communist hard-liners, his message was carried to the world by CNN.

In October of 1991, Ted delivered on a nearly two-decade old promise of a different kind when he brought baseball's World Series to Atlanta—the home of his Atlanta Braves team.

In December of 1991, Ted married Academy Award-winning actress, political activist, and exercise guru Jane Fonda.

At the end of the year, *Time* magazine named Ted its "Man of the Year." Ted, said *Time*, rewrote "the very definition of news...from something that has happened to something that is happening at the very moment you are hearing of it. A war involving the fiercest air bombardment in history unfolded in real time—before the cameras. The motherland of communism overthrew its leaders and their doctrine—before the cameras. To a considerable degree, especially in Moscow, momentous things happened precisely because they were being seen as they happened.

When Russian President Boris Yeltsin climbed on top of a tank to resist the attempted coup by hardline communists, CNN carried the images throughout the world.

These shots heard and seen around the world appeared under the aegis of the first global TV news company, Cable News Network."

For Ted Turner, 1991 was an extraordinary time. There have been other extraordinary years in the life of the man who turned a billboard company into one of the largest communications companies in the world. Along the way he has been called many things: crackpot, genius, playboy, sportsman, entrepreneur, fool, thrill seeker, crazy, cruel, and visionary. Ted might not disagree with any of these labels.

All these labels fit Ted at some point in his life. There is one trait, however, that has defined him his entire life. He is a survivor. Although he started life with many advantages, he had to overcome some terrible personal tragedies before he began building his financial empire. The forces that made Ted Turner the man he is, and that altered the shape of world media in the second half of the twentieth century, began shaping him from the beginning of his life.

Ted Turner has been called the "Mouth of the South." The irony of this label is that, although his father's family has southern roots, Ted himself was born in Cincinnati, Ohio.

The Turner family lived for generations near Sumner, Mississippi. Ted's grandfather lost most of his cotton land during the Great Depression of the 1930s. He opened a hardware store that Ted's father, Ed, was expected to work in after school.

Ed Turner attended the University of Mississippi for a while, but was forced to drop out because his father could no longer afford to pay his expenses. After leaving college, Ed moved north to Cincinnati and took a job in advertising. In Cincinnati, Ed met Florence Rooney, whose father owned the apartment building where he lived. They were married in 1937. Robert Edward Turner III was born on November 19, 1938. His parents called him Teddy.

In 1939, Ed Turner started a billboard company called Turner Outdoor Advertising. It was not the best time to start a billboard company. Two years later, the United States entered World War II, and the government imposed strict gas rationing that caused a steep decline in traveling. Companies with products to sell did not rent billboards because there were few drivers to see them.

Ted's sister, Mary Jean, was born in 1941. The same year three-year-old Teddy got in trouble for spreading mud over a neighbor's freshly washed white sheets as they hung drying on the line. He also pulled all the ornaments off the Christmas tree and crushed them.

In 1944, his business still declining, Ed went into the Navy. He was stationed on the Gulf Coast. Six-year-old Ted was sent to boarding school. Unable to get along at the school, Ted continued his pranks. He put stones in his classmates' galoshes and scrambled the clothes in their lockers. He was expelled.

After the war, Turner Advertising flourished. Ed bought two billboard companies in Savannah, Georgia, and moved his family south. At age nine, Ted was sent to the Georgia Military Academy in Atlanta. Ed thought the discipline at a military school would help Ted stop fighting and cutting up. It did not work. Years later, Ted remembered his first day at the school: "There were four of us in a little room, and right away I got into a fight with the biggest guy in the room and knocked the hell out of him. I sensed that if I didn't come out swinging they were going to kill me. That night, I said to my roommates, 'Who's the boss in here?' And I got the other three guys to go around saying I was the boss."

One day a rumor got started that the "new boy" from Cincinnati was bad-mouthing Robert E. Lee, the Confederate general. Soon, Ted was running for his life, pursued by a bloodthirsty platoon of about forty cadets brandishing a rope and screaming, "Kill the Yankee!" The next day, Ted became a highly visible Confederate sympathizer. His efforts to get along did not help, however. Before his first year was completed, Ed and the administration of the Georgia Military Academy decided that Ted should leave the school.

Ed Turner believed in hard work. Occasionally, he also drank too much alcohol and sometimes became abusive toward his

Ed Turner wanted his son to be insecure and willing to work hard.

son, whipping him with wire coat hangers and a razor. Ed wanted Ted to be obedient, but insecure, so he would grow up to be ambitious and work for everything he received. Ted had to cut the weeds from around the billboards, even the ones in swampy, snake-ridden locations.

During summer vacations, Ted escaped to his grandfather's Mississippi farm. He walked the creek beds catching toads and snakes, exploring rabbit warrens, and trapping turtles with a piece of string and a little hunk of meat.

Ed bought a yacht and joined the Savannah Yacht Club. He also bought a sailboat—a thirteen-foot plywood dinghy—for eleven-year-old Ted, who painted it black and called it "The Black Cat." Ted wanted to win every race he entered at the Savannah Yacht Club. The only problem was that he was not a very good sailor at first. His boat constantly filled with water. He became known as "Turnover Ted," the "Capsize Kid." But he eventually started to win—and that was all he cared about. He was trying to please Ed by being a winner and always being the leader. When he lost, he got little sympathy from his father. Ed thought sympathy made losers.

Clumsy at other sports, Ted grew proud of his sailing skill. He also loved to read fables and adventures and myths, to hike, fish and sail every chance he got. Often his father's African-American assistant, Jimmy Brown, spent his days out in the woods or on the water with Ted.

Ted managed to finish a whole year at the local public school. The next year, 1950, Ed decided again that Ted needed military school. This time he sent him to the McCallie Military Academy in Chattanooga, Tennessee. Ted hated the idea but he had no choice. He became the school's only seventh grade boarding student.

At McCallie, he became known as "Terrible Ted." He blew out all the electrical circuits and almost electrocuted himself when he tried to rearrange the lighting system in his room. He adopted all the homeless animals he could find—dogs, birds, gerbils, and snakes—despite the rules against having animals. Soon, he spent a great deal of time on punishment tours, which consisted of walking the oval track on a Saturday afternoon in full-dress uniform, carrying a wooden rifle. One honor code rule he always followed was to not lie. When asked, Ted always admitted to what he had done.

Ted could not hide the fact he hated going back to school after holidays. Maybe because of his loneliness at school, he became religious. At sermons, after the preachers talked about the unsaved burning in hell, Ted usually came forward during altar calls. His newfound religion got him to thinking about all the unsaved people in the world.

Ted was a C student. Ed considered these grades unacceptable. When he took Ted home for the summer after his first year at McCallie, he made Ted read classics and poetry. "I never

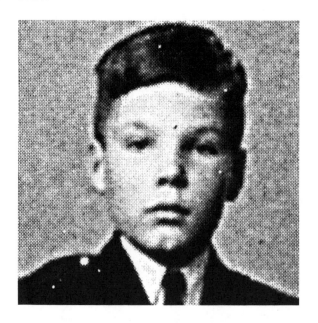

Ted was the only seventh grade boarding student at McCallie Military Academy.

considered not doing it," said Ted, "because I was instructed with wire coat hangers when I didn't get them read." When he wasn't reading, he was maintaining his father's billboards. Ed also charged Ted for his room and board to teach him how to handle his money. Meanwhile, his parents were always arguing bitterly, and his mother from time to time would threaten to move out.

Ted cut up for the next two years at McCallie. One spring evening, while sitting in the third-floor study hall, he climbed out the window when the proctor's head was turned, scrambled down the fire escape, went for a swim, bought a hamburger, and then climbed back up and in the window without being seen.

After his sister became ill, Ted dedicated himself to becoming a good cadet.

Ted eventually came to like McCallie. He became friends with his math teacher and taught the older man how to sail. The two then started a sailing club at the school. The school also had one long-term effect on Ted. Its rigid dinner and study schedule stuck with him. Even as an adult, he liked to have his meals at the same time every day.

Tragedy struck the Turner family when Ted was fifteen. His twelve-year-old sister, Mary Jean, to whom he had been close, developed a fatal form of a disease called lupus erythematosus. This disease tricks the body's immune system into attacking its own tissue.

Mary Jean suffered so much pain that she would cry out, "God, let me die, let me die." The family put her in a separate apartment over the garage with a full-time nurse.

"She was sweet as a little button. She worshipped the ground I walked on, and I loved her. A horrible illness," Ted said later. Mary Jean's illness made him bitter. Although he had been religious, and had even considered becoming a missionary, he now began having second thoughts about Christianity. He could not understand why God would let his sister suffer.

After Mary Jean became ill, Ted decided to change his attitude at McCallie. Suddenly, life was more serious. He began applying himself and became a voracious reader. "I read C.S. Forester's books, and Nordhoff and Hall about ten times—*Mutiny on the Bounty*, *Men Against the Sea*, and *Pitcairn's*

Ted (seated left) became an accomplished member of the McCallie debate team.

Island. I read about the War of 1812, and about the *Constitution*—you know, the ship. I remember reading the story of the Marines at Tripoli, and then I would go on to the dreadnoughts (battleships) in World War I, and then when I'd gone through that, on to World War II. My interest was always in why people did the things they did, and what caused some people to rise to glorious heights."

Ted liked to imagine himself as Alexander the Great. He memorized poetry and wrote some of his own, publishing one poem about sailing ships in the school paper. He joined the Debate Club and became a leader to the younger students. "In my junior year," he remembers, "I got to be an officer and an inspector—and then it was me who went around looking for dirt and giving other people demerits. But I always tried to be fair when I finally got into a leadership situation."

Winning a statewide debate was one high point of his senior year. The other was wearing his dress uniform—resplendent with gold braid, medals and gold chevrons—while at a formal dance with a coed from the nearby Girls Preparatory School.

Chapter Two

College Years

After graduating from McCallie, Ted went to Brown University, an ivy-league college in Providence, Rhode Island, after Harvard turned him down. Ed's graduation gift was an expensive new sailboat—but Ted would have to pay for half.

Ted felt out of place initially at Brown. "It mattered who your father was, how much money you had, what your clothes looked like," he remembers.

On his first day at Brown, he walked into his dorm room and announced to his new roommates: "I'm Ted Turner from Savannah. I'm the world's best sailor and the world's best lover."

Ted had trouble dealing with the switch from the structure of McCallie to the freedom of Brown. He barely managed to earn "C's" while playing poker, getting drunk every night, and sleeping through classes. He dated as many different girls as possible and sailed whenever he could on the nearby river. He loved to talk about himself and his successes and conquests, even if it meant waking up his roommates to do it. He argued politics constantly from a conservative point of view and never failed to defend the South. He also joined the sailing team and won often.

His first year at Brown was hectic and confusing. Back in Savannah for the summer, his parents finally divorced. Ted lived with his father. Ed's drinking had worsened. He sometimes disappeared for days, off on drunken binges.

In his sophomore year at Brown, Ted joined a fraternity where he continued drinking and gambling—and occasionally getting thrown in jail overnight. Once, he bet that he could drink an entire fifth of whiskey without stopping. He won the bet because he had already drunk a pint of olive oil to coat his stomach, but he still threw up.

Ted was often insensitive about people's feelings. He sang Nazi songs outside the Jewish fraternity house. And he put up warning signs from the Ku Klux Klan on the doors of the few black students in the dorm. His intention was to be funny. But the "jokes" were a problem because other students did not share his sense of humor.

Sailing was the one thing Ted took seriously. He knew more about sails and the wind than anyone else did. He won one meet in Chicago by sailing right over some ice that all the other teams were sailing around. The next year he was suspended from school for a semester after being arrested in a drunken ruckus outside a woman's dorm. He arrived in Savannah just in time to find out that his father was marrying again. The bride, Jane Dillard, was the pretty, graceful daughter of a socially prominent businessman. Ted was not thrilled about his father's remarriage, but he was pleasant to Jane.

Ed decided Ted should go into the Coast Guard Reserves. This way he could avoid being drafted, maybe learn some discipline, and be back at school in the fall. Ted enlisted in the Coast Guard in February of 1958 and served at the station in Cape May, New Jersey, for six months. Although he did very well, he was just as happy to be a civilian when he got out in September.

The next year, Ted was a sophomore again at Brown. He quickly returned to gambling, drinking, womanizing, and sailing. Sailing was a way for him to excel at something, since so many of his classmates came from fancy private prep schools and had been presidents of their classes, or football captains or academic stars.

Another drunken escapade landed Ted in jail for a few hours again until his fraternity brothers bailed him out. When he dated, he was mainly concerned about keeping score—how many girls he had gone out with, how many he had had sex with. He was copying his father once again.

Ted was barely passing his classes. But one course, in the classics (Latin and Greek) department, actually impressed him—he believed the professor had taught him how to think.

He even considered majoring in the classics rather than preparing for a business career, as his father wanted.

Ted told his father about his decision to change majors. Ed wrote him a long letter arguing against Ted majoring in the classics. Ed thought there was no reason to study something as old and as seemingly useless as Latin and Greek. Ted would be associating with "an isolated few impractical dreamers and a select group of college professors. God forbid!" Ed's letter made Ted angry. He thought it made Ed seem foolish. To prove his point, he had the letter published in the school paper, hoping others would agree that Ed was crude and lacked appreciation for education. But Ted gave up the classics and switched to economics. Ed was still the most powerful influence in his life. Ted barely passed his economic classes because, he says now, the teachers did not seem to believe in capitalism as strongly as he did.

Ted was kicked out of his fraternity for burning down its large papier-mâché display it had put up before the big football homecoming game.

When the school year ended, it was back to work for three more months at Turner Advertising, in the Savannah office. Ed had bought a thousand-acre cotton plantation he named Cotton Hall. The main house, built during the Depression, was as big as a mansion. Ted continued to sail on weekends or visit the new family home.

At Brown University, Ted could always find time to take a coed out sailing.

In his next, and last, year at Brown, Ted was sole captain of the sailing team. At the same Chicago race where he had triumphed so dramatically three years earlier by sailing over the ice, he met a woman captain, Judy Nye. She was sailing for the Northwestern University team. Ted immediately liked her and began a long-distance courtship.

Ted's time at Brown came to an end over Christmas. He was permanently expelled for having women in his dorm room.

Leaving Providence, Ted and a friend had grand plans to sail across the Atlantic. Then a lightning bolt toppled a tree on his boat and destroyed it. They decided to go to Florida to have fun.

Ted soon ran out of money and decided to go back into the Coast Guard to finish up his tour of duty. He spent most of the

Coast Guard time in Port Everglades, Florida, cheerfully cleaning the toilets and the bilge, the lowest level of the ship. His often-manic behavior drove everyone else crazy—until the captain said he was going to recommend Ted for the Coast Guard Academy. This was the last thing Ted wanted. He decided to settle down. He proposed to Judy. They were married in Chicago in the summer of 1960.

Not long after his wedding, Ted's sister, Mary Jean, died. She had suffered eight years of brain damage from encephalitis, a disease that resulted from her lupus. She had required intensive care at home for most of those years. Mary Jean was nineteen when she died.

Chapter Three

Taking Charge

Ed Turner was a big man with big appetites. He drank heavily and smoked three packs of cigarettes a day. In an effort to stop drinking and smoking, he took tranquilizers. Ed was also prone to intense and long depressions. He was always a hard, demanding parent, sometimes distant, sometimes even cruel, no matter how much Ted tried to please him.

After marrying Judy, Ted went to work for Turner Advertising. First he worked in Savannah, then Ed transferred him to the Macon, Georgia, office. In Macon, Ted began applying himself to business in a way that surprised those who had despaired at his inconsistent performance at school. He worked six- or seven-day weeks, often leaving the tiny apartment he shared with Judy before dawn and returning late at night. He joined most of the local business associations, such as the Chamber of Commerce and the Rotarians.

Despite Ted's best efforts, however, his father remained a man who was hard to please. Ted later told an interviewer: "I loved him. We loved each other, and yet we were so cruel. He was a hard man, and I tried to please him, although I didn't a lot of the time, and we had terrible, terrible fights."

Many of the difficulties Ted had in getting along with his father were because of Ed's increasing instability. The extent of Ed's emotional troubles soon became tragically clear.

In September 1962, Ed spent $4 million to buy the Atlanta, Richmond, and Roanoke divisions of the General Outdoor Advertising Company. This made Turner Outdoor Advertising the largest outdoor advertising company in the South. But Ed soon grew depressed and became convinced he had made a mistake. He entered into negotiations to sell his new purchase to a competitor, Naegele Advertising. Ted tried to talk him out of selling. It was no use. Ed's mind was made up.

During this period, Ed's drinking reached the point that he checked into a hospital for treatment. When he returned home, Ted saw a different man than the loud, strong-willed father he knew. Now Ed was a fearful ghost of his former self. When Ted tried to convince him to not follow through on the sale to Naegele, Ed refused to even argue with his son. Ted was shocked by what had happened to his father.

Then, in March 1963, Ed committed suicide at the family's newest plantation outside Savannah.

After the initial shock of losing his father, Ted assumed control of Turner Outdoor Advertising. He soon blossomed under the pressure. In the first risky business move of his life,

Ted with his father at the reception held after his marriage to Judy Nye.

Ted and Judy preparing to leave on their honeymoon.

he refused to go along with the commitment Ed had made to sell the new billboard purchases. He threatened the new owners that he would steal their employees and customers if they did not sell him back the businesses. He openly suggested that Naegele had taken advantage of his father's declining mental condition, and then flew to California and Minnesota and talked Naegele into returning the sold properties.

Naegele agreed, but with a dangerous condition. Ted would have to pay cash up front—cash he didn't have—and if he failed to pay off his loans, Naegele would take over all of Turner Outdoor Advertising. Ted would have to risk his entire company.

Ted with Judy, who is pregnant with their first child.

Ted thought that reversing his father's last business deal was a victory over the "big boys." To make it work, he sold the family plantations, collected all outstanding debts, and got an extension from Naegele. This was an important lesson he learned about himself: That even at age twenty-four he could hustle and deal with a crisis and come up a winner.

Years later, when asked why he hadn't just taken the money—he could have been a millionaire at twenty-four—Ted said: "My father had worked like hell all his life trying to make the big time. He went as far as he could, and when he dropped the baton, it was for me to pick it up. Plus, I am a fighter. I was raised that way. I could never be a dilettante living off the fat of the land. That business was really important to me. I don't know where I'd be without it."

In the next few years, Turner Outdoor Advertising grew at a rapid clip. Ted bought out competitors in Knoxville and Chattanooga, Tennessee, and began to consolidate his hold on the entire South. He built the South's largest outdoor sign in Atlanta and wired it to light up at night.

Ted social life continued at the fast pace that had driven him out of Brown. He worked hard and partied harder. Ted was still emulating many of his father's habits. This included being unfaithful to Judy. Eventually, she tired of being at home with their children, Laura Lee and Robert Edward Turner IV (Teddy), while Ted was either working or out on the town with other women. Judy asked for a divorce.

Although his marriage to Judy had lasted only two years, Ted persuaded her to sail with him. They had won a national championship the summer of 1963, only months after his father's death. He told her he wanted to continue their on-water partnership, but he was clearly interested in remarriage. Judy tried to decide if she should go back to Ted. Jimmy Brown, now Ted's assistant, took care of the kids on weekends while they sailed.

Ted and Judy broke up for good in the spring of 1964. The incident that convinced her she could not live with him came during a one-person-boat race. When it appeared that she was going to win, Ted rammed her boat to deny her the victory. Judy took the children and went back to Chicago.

After the final split with Judy, Ted began dating women in his new home, Atlanta. Women found him attractive. He was tall—six feet, two inches—handsome, blue-eyed and prematurely graying. He soon met and became engaged to Jane Smith, an attractive flight attendant. They married in June 1964, after his usual intense courtship.

"I couldn't for the life of me see why he was interested anyhow, we were so different," Jane said later. "I thought he was crazy. But there was no getting away, even though once I let the phone ring all day long without taking it off the hook. He was always bragging about this and that. He finally wore me down."

Jane also remembered that during this time he was bored with his job at Turner Outdoor Advertising. After the initial period of tension, when he had to save the company or lose it to his competitor, the billboard companies were running smoothly. On some days he slept until ten-thirty or eleven o'clock in the morning.

Ted and Jane had three children in the next five years. Rhett was named for Rhett Butler in the novel, *Gone With The Wind.* Beauregard was named for the confederate general. His new daughter was named Jennie. Ted's children from his marriage to Judy Nye, Laura Lee and Teddy, came to live with them later.

As Ted grew bored with the billboard business, sailing became even more of an obsession. He entered a race nearly every weekend. He also became a more ambitious sailor. He had started out with eleven-foot Penguin sailboats. Now he moved up to seventy-foot ocean racers. Then he was ready for the most famous sailboats of all—the twelve-meter yachts that competed for the America's Cup, the premier event in sailing.

The large boats required larger crews. Ted was every inch the captain. He won more often than he lost, usually by pushing his crew not to sleep or rest. He loved every moment of racing. "Some races are so beautiful that you're sorry to finish," he said later. "The Montego Bay race in '66 was one. It was a full moon, clear nights, warm, and there was a good wind. The world was beautiful. In our sport, you're out there with nature—you're as

Ted, every bit the captain, loved the world of yacht racing.

close to nature as you can be—with gulls, flying fish, whales, the dawn, the sunset, the stars. You take a deep breath and you feel alive, really alive. The brilliance of the stars is hard to describe. You think you can reach out and grab a handful of them. It's as if they're ten feet away, and there are millions of them."

In 1967 he and a crew sailed across the Atlantic to Copenhagen, the capital of Denmark. They nearly sank several times. Ted climbed the mast to make repairs in the middle of storms.

Jane remembered what happened after Ted arrived in Denmark: "Ted had arranged to be in another regatta in Copenhagen. King Constantine of Greece was sailing—I remember his high boots and the wonderful jackets that he wore. Prince Juan Carlos of Spain was there for the races too, and King Olaf of Norway, who's a wonderful man."

From 1964 to 1969 Ted put in more time at the helm than most sailors do in a lifetime. He assembled highly dedicated groups of men who were as committed to racing as he was. He would have someone else sail his boats to the starting line so he could fly in and start the race immediately, without worrying about supplies or other details.

He sailed in as many as a dozen major races around the world each year from 1964 to 1980. In the summer of 1970, he won a race off the coast of Florida, flew for sixteen hours to Australia for a race, then flew back in time for the next Florida race.

In the winter of 1967-68 Ted chartered a yacht and went to Long Island to sail it. The harbor was frozen, however, and Ted had to rent an oceangoing tug to break a path to open water.

The night before they were to leave Long Island, the yacht sank. The crew pumped her out, and they managed to sail out of the harbor. Then they got caught in a winter storm off the coast of Cape Hatteras, North Carolina, and realized the boat was still leaking. Cape Hatteras is one of the most dangerous places in the world for boats, because of its treacherous shoals.

The crew formed bucket brigades to dump water overboard. The mainsail broke and the engine failed. Ted radioed the Coast Guard for help, who radioed a tanker to stand by. Two men were washed overboard, but were saved by their safety harnesses. Somehow the boat avoided the rocks and was finally towed into Morehead City, North Carolina, where they made repairs and sailed the next day. Amazingly, they got to their destination in time for the first race on the Southern Ocean Racing Circuit off the coast of Miami. Ted's boat won the race, and it was the start of a series of yearly victories on the racing circuit.

Ted decided to compete in the America's Cup racing and bought the *American Eagle*, a boat that had lost in previous America's Cups.

In 1969 Ted sailed in the World Ocean Racing Championship, eighteen races all over the world. He had to sail in at least seven races in a three-year period to maintain membership. This kept him busy. By 1970 he had competed in Ireland, Jamaica, Bermuda, Denmark, Norway, Australia, and Hawaii. He was winning regularly, though for his crewmen it meant screaming, insults and occasionally punches.

In 1970 Ted was named Yachtsman of the Year. He received the honor twice more, in 1973 and 1977.

Chapter Four

Superstation

By 1968, Turner Outdoor Advertising was the fifth largest billboard company in the nation. But, for Ted, billboards were merely a means to an end. He wanted to create a business empire.

Ted decided to get into broadcasting. He bought a radio station in Chattanooga, Tennessee. He learned a valuable lesson buying the station, one he would never forget. He told the original station owners that he wanted to think over their price, only to discover the next day that they had sold to someone else half an hour after he left. Ted phoned the new owner and offered him a higher price and bought the station. It was an expensive way to learn to make quick decisions.

The new radio station was at the bottom in its market. Its programs included a preacher who opened fund-raising envelopes on the air so listeners could hear coins falling on the table. Someone else played a bugle. The station covered golf matches live, which, of course, the listeners could not see. Ted changed the station to a Top 40 hits format and advertised it on any of his available billboards.

Using one part of his business to promote another part was to become the key strategy to Ted's success. Years before the buzzword *synergy* was being thrown around in management circles, Ted hit on the idea of growing his corporation by letting one part of his business hold up another until it could stand on its own feet. He followed this pattern through most of his career.

Ted bought another station in Jacksonville, Florida, two in Charleston, South Carolina, and another in Chattanooga. He borrowed to finance these purchases, confident that his vision of how to grow Turner Advertising was sound.

Ted bought his first television station almost accidentally. He seldom watched television. As far as he was concerned, television was just another way to advertise. A banker, anxious to sell a little-watched Atlanta UHF station with a weak signal, proposed that Ted buy it. After very little analysis, Ted put his billboard company profits at risk to buy the station. Many of the men who worked in management at Turner Outdoor Advertising advised against the move. A few even quit, convinced that Ted was going to bankrupt the company.

Ted explains his sudden business decisions this way: "I don't believe in marketing studies. Do you want to do it? Are you committed to making it work? Then it will, or at least it'll have the only chance it ever had. The reason nothing gets done in this country anymore is that there are so many committees. It just has to be you."

The station was so poorly supplied they had to trade advertising for furniture. Sometimes they were off the air for long periods when the equipment failed. Ted says of that period: "I just love it when people say I can't do something. There's nothing that makes me feel better, because all my life people have said I wasn't going to make it."

The station couldn't afford to rent color movies, so they showed old black and white ones—and he got to know the people in the film business. In the days before the VCR was in most homes, Ted realized that if he bought old films, rather than rent them, he could make his money back many times by simply showing them over and over. Later, he bought a second television station, a bankrupt one in Charlotte, North Carolina. He bought this one with his own money. This station continued to do poorly and was soon bleeding him dry. He had to go on the air and use all of his charm to solicit money from viewers. He also began selling off his smaller outdoor advertising companies to keep his television stations running.

Ted knew he needed to improve programming and expand the viewing audience. Things did not turn around until he began a strategy called counter-programming. This consisted of running completely different types of shows to draw the audience that did not want to watch what was on other stations. Ted counter-programmed with reruns of old network shows like "Star Trek," "Gilligan's Island," "Leave It To Beaver," "The Beverly Hillbillies," "Petticoat Junction," "Gomer Pyle," and "The Andy Griffith Show." Ted loved to counter-program the other stations' local and network news shows. Ted hated the news. He thought it was depressing and boring and was convinced many others agreed with him. This turned out to be one of his best decisions. Many viewers preferred situation comedy reruns to world events.

Ted also loaded the schedule with professional wrestling, "Roller Derby," and old feature films. One of his best moves was to take advantage of the local NBC affiliate's decision to not air several network programs. Ted bought the programs and announced on his billboards that NBC had moved to his channel.

In 1973, Ted contracted to show Atlanta Braves baseball games on his stations. At that time, the Braves were the only major league baseball team in the southeastern United States. He knew there was a market for the games well outside the metropolitan Atlanta area. If he could start attracting this wide audience, he could increase the rates he charged to advertisers.

Ted changed the Atlanta station's name to WTCG and began referring in advertising to it as the "Superstation." The strategy was a success; station viewership grew. Despite losing most of their games, the Braves were hugely popular. Advertisers began flocking to the station. As viewership grew, WTCG sold advertising time to products that could be ordered over the phone or through the mail—such things as recordings of old country hits, mood rings, "genuine" family coats of arms, pocket size fishing rods, and kitchen knives that could cut through a can.

During these years Ted was so busy that he saw little of his family. Often, the only way for his family to see him was to tune in "Academy Award Theatre" on Sunday mornings, where Ted was the taped host.

Late in 1974, Ted became fascinated with the idea of using a satellite to beam his television station's signal around the country. That had never been done before. Up to that point, the television networks used power lines to send their signals to local TV stations. With the aid of a powerful transmitter—an uplink—WTCG could beam the Braves to a satellite orbiting the earth 23,000 miles in space. In less than a second, the signal would be beamed to dish-shaped receivers owned by cable television companies all over the U.S. It was static-free and relatively cheap transmission, compared to landlines and microwave.

Ted, who always had less cash than ideas, could pay for his uplink by charging cable companies ten cents for each one of their subscribers. It took a year of negotiations and several refusals from lenders before the money for the complicated setup was raised.

WTCG, the "Superstation," was beamed to the satellite on December 17, 1976. The signal was seen from Honolulu to the Virgin Islands, Mexico City to Maine, Alaska to Canada. WTCG began with links to cable systems in twenty-seven states.

Selling advertising on a satellite station wasn't easy. Though national in scope, few homes were yet wired for cable and the audience was small. But, as usual, Ted's strategic thinking was sound and foresighted. He was essentially doing an end run around the networks—ABC, CBS and NBC—and their huge investment in landlines. But in the short term, the "Superstation" could survive only by offering an alternative to viewers. Unfortunately, the advertisers were slower than Ted to recognize the great potential in cable.

Ted had no choice but to hit the road and sell the concept to the people with the money. "Turner would do anything to sell his station to advertisers," remembers one associate. "He'd jump up on chairs, on desks, on tables, on anything that didn't move, and shout at the top of his larynx. If he met really serious resistance, he might even drop to the floor as if he'd been shot and cry, 'You're killin' me!'" He usually persuaded advertising agencies to buy time on his stations by dropping his prices. Not many people were watching, but the price was right.

During this time, Ted continued to rail against the news. He made no money from news broadcast, but the Federal Communications Commission required stations to carry the news. His stations presented the minimum amount required. The news at Ted's "Superstation" came on at three in the morning, and it was played for laughs. Anchorman Bill Tush would read the Associated Press wire reports with a German Shepherd as his co-anchor. The dog, wearing a shirt and tie, chewed a mouthful of peanut butter and seemed to be reading the day's events along with Tush. On one occasion, Tush donned a gorilla suit to announce a "guerrilla" attack; on another, he cut to downtown Atlanta for a report from the "Unknown Announcer," a co-worker with a microphone and a paper bag over his head. This was a curious beginning for the future founder of the Cable News Network.

Ted made up most of his programming as he went along. "I programmed the whole station myself in those days," he remembered later. "I sold ads, I signed all the payroll checks, I went to parties. I met people, I asked a million stupid questions and I educated myself. I would wander around in a daze all day, thinking, What am I gonna put on at four-thirty? No committees, no studies, no bull. I would ask Janie what she thought of a certain movie, or one of my friends, or the girls at the office. Not too scientific, huh?"

In 1976, Ted bought the money-losing Atlanta Braves to make sure their games would remain available for his station. He figured he could lose $5 million a year on the team and still

After he bought the Atlanta Braves, Ted became the team's biggest fan.

break even because the games were popular programming. Baseball games also run long, providing time to sell plenty of ads. Eventually, due to the greater exposure he gave the team, the Braves became one of the most profitable franchises in baseball.

After watching the team on television, viewers of the "Superstation" who lived in other areas of the country were anxious to go to Braves games when possible. Again, Ted was employing his strategy of using one part of his company to develop the other.

Ted hung around the training camp and the players and began to learn about a game he had little understanding of before. He even took up chewing tobacco like the players and coaches—though all the spitting made his clothes dirty. To promote the team, he made a singing commercial with his players, swinging a bat while he urged viewers to "come on out and see the Braves at your Atlanta teepee." Before games, he would roam the halls of WTCG with a cap on his head and a bat on his shoulder. He sat in a seat behind the Braves dugout, drinking beer and rooting for the team. He sometimes, usually after drinking too much beer, even ran out on the field to lead the crowd in singing "Take Me Out To The Ball Game."

When a Braves' player hit the team's first home run of the 1976 season, Ted leaped over the fence and raced to greet the hitter at home plate. The fans loved having an enthusiastic local

In an effort to attract fans to the Braves games, Ted competed in an ostrich race.

boy as owner. But when the Braves lost that same game, he kicked a wall so hard he nearly broke his foot.

During the tenth game of a long losing streak, Ted took the place of one of the pretty girls in short shorts that swept the bases during the seventh inning. During the same slump, he brought in a minister to pray for the team. After the twelfth consecutive loss, he lay "in state" on top of the dugout with his hands folded on his chest.

Ted threw himself into baseball, traveling to all the National League ballparks, meeting the general managers, and discussing every aspect of the baseball business. He learned an enormous amount quickly. He involved himself in every aspect of Braves management, even dressing as a batboy and a manager. He had a sharp eye for waste and fired several of the team's management personnel for spending too much money.

Ted was determined that even if the team didn't win, at least fans would have a good time. There was a giant TV screen on the scoreboard, and Ted held "Gourmet Days," "Bartender Days" and "Ladies' Days." There were ostrich races and home-plate weddings, Easter egg hunts and dollar-bill scrambles, mattress stacking and motorized bathtub competitions. Ted organized free-halter-top giveaways and had an aerialist in a Braves cap do a skywalk 200 feet above the infield. He presented fireworks, wrestling matches and belly dancers. He raced in the ostrich race and stacked mattresses himself. Once,

Ted was willing to do almost anything to promote the Atlanta Braves.

he pushed a baseball with his nose around the infield in a race with a Philadelphia Phillies player. He won the race, but bloodied his nose and forehead so severely the wounds took weeks to heal.

The people of Atlanta began a love affair with the local "loudmouth" entrepreneur. His name and face were constantly in newspapers and magazines all over the country. Ted enjoyed the notoriety of being written about in *Time, Sports Illustrated* and *Playboy*. He appeared on the cover of *Sports Illustrated* that summer and sent an autographed copy to baseball commissioner Bowie Kuhn.

Ted's antics endeared him to the fans, but the baseball

commissioner disapproved. He warned Ted to control himself. Then Ted made what Kuhn considered an improper job offer to a player for the San Francisco Giants. Kuhn suspended Ted from baseball for a year.

Atlanta came to Ted's defense. The mayor and local businessmen presented Kuhn with a petition signed by ten thousand people. But the commissioner was not impressed. Ted even sued in federal court to break the suspension, but to no avail. The ban was upheld.

Ted also had bought the Atlanta Hawks basketball team. He said they were the "world's two worst sports franchises."

Chapter Five

America's Cup

The New York Yacht Club, the sponsor of the America's Cup races, did not want Ted as a member. The membership committee thought he was a crude redneck. The America's Cup is strictly for the rich, preferably the old-money rich. Ted was the worst kind of new money. However, as he continued to rack up victory after victory on the sailing circuit, they soon had no choice. Ted became a member in 1973.

The summer of 1973, Ted was in Oslo, Norway, for a race on July 13, on the Isle of Wight off Great Britain on July 26, at Sardinia off Italy on August 25, at Malta off Italy on September 28. He would fly home between races while the crew sailed to the next site. He calculated that it was costing him $100,000 a year—$20,000 in plane tickets alone. This was a typical summer for him.

Win or lose, the one thing Ted and his crew could be sure of was exhaustion. According to a writer who has sailed with him, "After an ocean race, hands will be swollen from the constant hauling of wet lines. Shoulders will ache from grinding winches. Knees and elbows will be sore from scampering across nonskid decks. Fingers will be chafed and raw from handling salt-soaked Dacron sails. There will be assorted bruises and cuts and occasional serious injuries."

Said the same writer of the captain: "Ted Turner knows his boat with intimacy. He knows what the boat will do when and how and under what conditions."

In 1974, Ted competed in the trials set to select the American boat and crew that would defend the America's Cup. In this competition a series of races are run to select the best yacht to sail for the United States in the international competition. Ted's ship lost badly and had to be rebuilt. Then his tactician, Dennis Conner, replaced him as skipper.

This was a tough time for Ted—he wasn't used to losing. The America's Cup trials were held off the coast of Newport, Rhode Island. Janie and the kids were in Newport that summer, but they never saw him. Jimmy Brown instructed the kids in sailing, just as he had Ted when he was a boy.

After the season, Ted tried to buy the *Courageous,* the boat that had won the cup, in anticipation of the next competition in 1977. He thought that if he owned the best racing boat he would have to be considered as the boat to defend the title. But the owners turned him down.

In 1977, as Ted's troubles with Major League Baseball were

in the headlines, Ted was being invited back into America's Cup racing. The same people who had resisted extending him a membership now needed his money to finance a radically new aluminum boat design. Ted initially declined their invitation because he would not get to sail the fastest current boat, the *Courageous*, which had won the cup in the last competition. Now, he offered money for the aluminum design on condition of a chance to buy and sail *Courageous*, no matter how well the new boat did. This time his offer was accepted.

Ted was confident of winning the America's Cup this time, with a proven boat, an experienced crew and determination.

In the qualifying races, *Courageous* won seven of its eight races. Then the *Courageous* started to lose. Now Ted saw himself in his classic fashion, as the underdog.

In the next race, Ted was pitted against the *Enterprise*. The *Enterprise* jumped out ahead. "The noise aboard *Courageous* was astonishing, given that it was being driven by wind rather than internal combustion," wrote a crew member. "There was the jangle of metal on metal, the flapping of sails, the pounding of the hull on the water, the excited shouts of the angry captain." They passed *Enterprise* in the last part of the race and won.

Janie and the kids were in Newport during the races, although Ted did not spend much time with them. Ted was frenetic, on or off the water, flirting with pretty women, drinking in bars, getting kicked out of restaurants for drunkenness, and generally angering the wealthy yachtsmen who lived in Newport.

But on board the *Courageous,* Ted was all business. *Courageous* won all but one of its races in August, and was selected to defend the America's Cup against a ship named *Australia.*

To celebrate his victory, Ted had T-shirts printed with a picture of him with the caption "Captain Courageous." President Jimmy Carter congratulated him and invited him to dinner at the White House, where he was singled out for praise. Ted had single-handedly made this sport for sailors into a big event for the media.

Huge crowds turned out for the first race against the *Australia* in mid-September. *Courageous* won, and won the second in an exciting duel. Ted's mother was there. He won the third race by a huge margin, and the fourth and last the same way. A cannon blast signaled final victory. Ted had won the America's Cup, the premier event in yacht racing. An armada of yachts and ferries and boats of every size and shape followed them toward the wharf.

Tossing the victors into the harbor water was traditional. Ted was the first thrown in. He had fortified himself for the dunking with champagne. Afterwards, he ran around the dock spraying water on everyone. He drank from two liquor bottles at the same time on national television during the post-race news con-

Ted is carried off by his crew after winning the 1977 America's Cup.

ference. Then, after he had thanked everybody, his crew carried him off on their shoulders. The last thing Ted said that night before falling asleep was, "Wouldn't the old man be proud of me tonight?"

In 1980 Ted went back to Rhode Island to defend the America's Cup. This time one of his competitors would be Dennis Connor, who had been sailing daily and winning races. Connor was one of the new breed of yacht racer, the professional captain. He was able to devote all his time to preparing for races while Ted was clearly distracted by all his business concerns. Ted had been sailing for only fifty days during the previous year, while Connor was all business.

Ted lost most of his races in June and July. He lost his final race to Connor on August 5 and was out of competition. The professional had beaten the amateur, and sailing had changed. Shortly thereafter, Ted renounced competitive sailing altogether and sold both of his boats, *Courageous* and *Tenacious*. He confined himself to racing an eighteen-foot catamaran with son Rhett crewing.

Chapter Six

Chicken Noodle Network

In the months after his 1977 victory in the America's Cup race, Ted began working on the idea that eventually won him worldwide fame: a twenty-four-hour television news station. It would be called the Cable News Network and would take advantage of satellite, cable and videotape technology. A two-hour news show, divided into national, financial, women-oriented and sports news sections, would be repeated and updated throughout the day.

Ted was not the first to think of a continuous, satellite-fed news channel. Twenty-four hour news radio had been a feature of most large media markets for years. Other television entrepreneurs, such as Gerard Leven, who started Home Box Office (HBO) and Reese Schonfeld, who worked with Ted on CNN, had also kicked around the idea. But Ted was the first to dedicate himself to making it work.

For those who knew Ted, the joke was that he had always been hostile to the news. The "Superstation" still had Bill Tush doing news in the middle of the night that occasionally featured "updates" on the progress of the studio's new linoleum floor.

In November of 1978, Ted contacted his old friend, independent TV news producer Reese Schonfeld and pitched his plan for a cable news network. The call lasted thirty seconds and went like this:

"Reese, How're ya doin'?"

"I'm fine, Ted. How are you?"

"I'm thinking about doing twenty-four hours of news for cable. Can it be done?"

"Yes."

"Do you want to do it?"

"Yes."

"Come on down and see me."

Atlanta would be a much cheaper place for a headquarters than New York. Labor costs were much cheaper in Georgia, a non-union state. Ted needed to find ways to save all the money that he could. Unlike the big networks, there would be no backup revenues earned from an entertainment division. The networks had never considered their news divisions to be profit centers. The traditional attitude was that news provided prestige to a network. Money was made through the entertainment divisions. Ted was attempting to make an entire network totally dependent on news for its profitability.

Ted had been looking for a way to grow in the now fast-

Reese Schonfeld organized the creation of CNN.

growing cable industry. HBO had beaten him to become the first broadcast movie channel, ESPN carried twenty-four-hour sports. News was all that was left.

Estimates were that it would cost $100 million to get started, and that it would take at least three years before ad and cable subscription money could start covering costs. Profits were years away, if ever.

One thing Ted did not concern himself about was the fact he knew nothing about journalism. As he explained it, "I didn't know anything about radio when I bought my radio stations, and I didn't know anything about television when I bought my TV stations. I've got a real fast learning curve. I always rely on being able to learn stuff. Experts are the easiest thing there are to hire."

Raising the money for the all-news station, which would be subsidized by his other businesses, was slow going. No one believed he could do it.

Ted would not be put off. He felt there was a need for an in-depth news channel. As he explained to one interviewer at the time: "Television news just hasn't been doing its job. This country is in trouble, and all you hear about is the surface stuff—rapes, murders, fires in abandoned buildings. I don't know much about it but I know it stinks. Every night we watch anchormen on the news who look like they know what's going on, and then the Arabs give us an oil crisis and it takes us by surprise. It's just totally irresponsible. But I'm doing something about it. I'm going to prove there's room for competition in the country, even if I go broke doing it."

As CNN was just getting off the ground, another venture of Ted's was finally seeing some success. His NBA team, the Atlanta Hawks, had become central division champs. Ted invited President Carter to one of the playoff games outside Washington, and Carter flew Ted and Janie up in Air Force One—a first for them both. The only problem was that Ted was losing money on the Hawks every year.

His cable station, WTCG—soon to be WTBS—was being seen on more and more cable systems. He was now able to charge national rates as advertisers realized what kind of audience they could reach. This profit center made his other ventures possible.

Ted decided he had reached the go-ahead point for CNN in May of 1979. He told Schonfeld to start readying CNN for broadcast. Schonfeld planned to put on real news, like the networks, only all the time—and frequently live. Ted also signed the highly respected newsman Daniel Schorr, who had formerly worked for CBS, as his senior Washington correspondent. Ted admitted later that he had never heard of Daniel Schorr before offering him the job. He had briefly considered trying to hire Dan Rather, though he'd never heard of him, either. Also signed were political commentators Bella Abzug, Phyllis Schlafly, Rowland Evans, Robert Novak, and psychologist Joyce Brothers. The format would mix standard, but longer, newscasts with breaking news and live coverage. He had found a headquarters building—a former country club in Atlanta.

Ted announced to the public that CNN would begin broadcasting on June 1, 1980. The announcement was made from a May 1979 news conference at a Las Vegas cable convention.

While the convention was still going on, Ted returned to sailing, taking sixteen-year-old Teddy to crew for him on the *Tenacious*. With seventeen other crewmembers, they sailed in the 600-mile Fastnet race between England and Ireland.

During the Fastnet, hurricane winds scattered the boats, sank some, and killed fifteen sailors. Schonfeld was working on a newsroom set for CNN when he heard that Turner's boat was missing. But Ted not only had survived the storm—he won the race.

Ironically, the race illustrated what CNN was to be all about. Dan Schorr turned on a network newscast and heard a dated story about Ted being missing. But then he heard, almost immediately, that Ted was alive. As Schorr told cable conventioneers a few minutes later, "The reason you might have thought he was still missing is because you were looking at old-fashioned television, which is delayed across the country. And that's one thing CNN won't do, because it's being carried live everywhere."

Ted started personally promoting CNN in late 1979. The first staff had been hired, including newscaster Bernard Shaw and producers. Most of the newly hired, lowly-paid staff were so inexperienced, though, that the joke was soon being whispered that the letters CNN meant "Chaos News Network."

Reese Schonfeld realized there was only one way he could make his small budget cover all the different kinds of jobs at the network: have everybody do everything. He even coined a name for his new employees: Vee-Jay, or VJ, for "video journalist." This sharing of tasks was only possible because the staff were non-union. Recently graduated journalism students worked long days for near minimum wage to learn the trade.

Then, in December 1979, the satellite slated to carry CNN's

Ted and his then-wife Jane with President Jimmy Carter in the White House.

signal was lost in space shortly after launch. After an intense meeting in New York, that occasionally deteriorated into a screaming match, Ted persuaded RCA to give him temporary access to another satellite.

CNN hoped to make money from selling advertising and by charging each cable system that carried its programming twenty cents per subscriber, fifteen cents if the system also carried the Superstation. The cable companies would also be able to sell two of the twelve available advertising minutes per hour.

CNN began broadcasting right on schedule on June 1, 1980, at 6 p.m. There was an opening ceremony in front of the redesigned headquarters. Ted used three flagpoles to symbolize the view of the world he wanted CNN to represent. "You'll notice that out in front of me we've raised three flags," he told the crowd. "One is of the state of Georgia, where we're located. In the center, the flag of the United States, which represents the nation this Cable News Network intends to serve. On the other side is the flag of the United Nations, because we hope with our greater depth, and our international coverage, to make possible a better understanding of how people from different nations can live and work, and so to bring together in brotherhood and kindness and peace the people of this nation and world."

Then a switch was thrown, and the new anchors started reading the news. Their images appeared on televisions from Hawaii to Boston in two million American homes.

The first news item was a report of the shooting of civil rights activist Vernon Jordan in Fort Wayne, Indiana. There was a live feed from the hospital. President Carter was seen saying that his old friend appeared to be recovering. CNN had to interrupt its very first commercial, for an anti-acid, to cover the story.

Minutes later, the feed switched abruptly to the Middle East and then to Key West, Florida. Ted had made good on his promise of instant news from anywhere, via satellite.

There were frequent problems at first. Satellite pictures appeared without sound, or sound appeared without pictures. The anchor then apologized to the viewers and kept on. But even the glitches sent the message that what the viewer was watching was immediate, raw news, without the slick polish they were used to from the big three networks. Also, the news did not end each day—it was continuous. A CNN reporter could stay with a story, and the network could cut back to it at any time—or even run it as a tiny box in a corner of the viewer's screen.

What was not so visible to the viewers was the small size of the CNN staff—fewer than each of the major networks employed in Washington, D.C., alone.

At first, critics called CNN the "Chicken Noodle Network" for its inexperience and rough edges. There were plenty of problems. Once, someone noted, "a lightbulb exploded and set Dan Schorr's clothes on fire while he was reporting live from Washington. . . a cleaning woman walked past Bernard Shaw's desk as he delivered the news and proceeded to empty his wastebasket while America watched. . . weatherman Stu Siroka almost got swallowed up in the revolving panels of his weather map...anchors found themselves on the air fumbling with news copy, mangled copy or no copy at all. . . ."

In the beginning, Ted lost at least $1 million a month on CNN. Few national advertisers were signing on, and not all the cable systems signed up. Ted had pledged his entire personal fortune and everyone expected him to fail.

What Ted's detractors did not understand was that the satellite would change the way the news was reported—giving it immediacy it had rarely had before. CNN would stay with a story like the 1980 Mt. St. Helens eruption in Washington or the political conventions that summer when the older networks were moving on to other stories.

To boost viewership, Ted started promoting not just CNN but cable viewing itself. He also attacked the networks, sometimes by using outrageous language that said they promoted crime with their alleged sensationalism. "In the race for ratings, their newscasts dig up the most sordid things human beings do or the biggest disasters and try to make them seem as exciting as possible," he claimed. "In their entertainment programs, they make heroes of criminals and glamorize violence. They've polluted our minds and our children's minds. I think they're almost guilty of manslaughter.

Ted announced the launching of CNN on June 1, 1980.

"What those networks are doing is making Hitler Youth out of the American people—lazy, drug addicts, homosexuals, sex maniacs, materialists, disrespectful. I mean, you know—mockery of their parents, mockery of all the institutions. It's bad. Bad, bad, bad! They oughta be tried for treason; they're the worst enemies America's ever had." The cable operators loved this kind of ludicrous attack. They saw the networks as their enemy. They began rewarding Ted for carrying their fight by signing up to receive CNN.

Ted began sleeping at the headquarters, trying to figure out how to save it financially. He considered a merger with one of the major networks, even as he denounced them in public. He had a secret meeting at CBS in September of 1981 to discuss the possibility of the network buying CNN. But he would consider a sale only on his terms. He was determined not to share control of his company. This was a condition no network would meet. There would be other meetings with networks through the early 1980s, but no one made a firm offer for his company. It soon became clear that if CNN was going to be successful, it would have to do it on its own.

In 1981 CNN was the only network to carry split-screen coverage of President Ronald Reagan's inauguration in Washington and of the release of the U.S. hostages who had been held in Iran for over a year. Despite this accomplishment, it was not until the next year, and only after the threat of a lawsuit, that

CNN gained equal participation in the White House press pool.

To capture the attention of Congress, Ted donated a satellite dish to the U.S. House of Representatives and wired all the representatives' offices. (Washington D.C. was not wired for cable at the time.) One CNN employee explained their strategy this way: "Part of [our success] is just being on twenty-four hours a day. Members of Congress and Washington leaders would be watching CNN at two in the morning because it was the only thing on."

1981 was the do or die year for CNN and—because Ted had risked all of his personal and corporate money on the venture—Turner Broadcasting. The biggest problem was that CNN was under-funded. Although he had risked everything, there was not enough money to keep it running for a year. By 1982, the revenues generated by the Superstation should be enough to carry CNN until it made a profit. But, until then, CNN needed to generate more money.

Ted increased his efforts to sell advertising and to convince cable system operators all over the country to carry CNN. It was often a hard sell because most cable operators did not believe CNN would survive. They all read the same reports in the broadcast trade journals that predicted CNN's death.

At this desperate time Ted received even more bad news. The giant broadcasting company ABC and the multinational corporation Westinghouse announced that they would join together to form the Satellite News Channel. This new service would consist of thirty-minute newscasts, repeated throughout the day and night.

Most observers did not think that ABC or Westinghouse was very interested in creating a viable cable news channel. Instead, the goal seemed to be to destroy CNN, which ABC saw as a direct threat to its network news service. The two companies were worth an estimated $4 billion, while Turner Broadcasting was valued at only $200 million. It looked like the large companies were working together to crush the tiny upstart.

Ted's reaction to this threat was no surprise to the people who worked for him in Atlanta, or to those who had been observing him over the years. He called his management team into his office at CNN headquarters and announced that they were starting a sister station, CNN II (the name was changed later to Headline News) that would follow the same format as the Satellite News Channel. But, instead of taking a year to get the new service on the air, CNN II would premiere in six months. "It's a preemptive first strike!" Ted crowed. "They [ABC and Westinghouse] have only money to lose, but we have every-thing to lose." Later, Ted went on CNN to attack ABC and Westinghouse. "The only way they're gonna get rid of me is to put a bullet in me!" he yelled.

Ted's tough talk could not change the fact that CNN risked not making it through the year. Although CNN II would use the same reporters and tape that was used on its sister network, it would still cost several million dollars to build new studios and to hire people to run the operation. Ted, however, thought he had no choice. If the large national advertisers he was struggling to sign up on CNN thought that the new Satellite News Channel was going to force him off the air he would have no chance to sell them advertising. The only way to save CNN was to convince these advertisers, such as automobile manufacturers and household product companies, that CNN would be around the next year and the year after that. Ted, the classic entrepreneur, saw no choice but to keep on going. To not continue being aggressive meant sure death for Turner Broadcasting.

When the Satellite News Channel went live in June of 1982 they announced they would not be charging the subscribers to receive the signal. This meant Ted could not charge for Headline News. This placed Turner Broadcasting in such a fragile position that Ted began offering deep discounts to advertisers if they would pay in advance. On more than one occasion, Ted was unable to meet the entire payroll. He kept most of his employees working by delivering a series of pep talks and by traveling the country wildly in search of money.

One central advantage Ted had over his larger rivals was that he did not have as many people to question his judgement. He did not have to receive the blessing of stockholders to keep going because he still owned the controlling interest in his company. The only people he had to convince were bankers, advertisers and employees. ABC and Westinghouse had to justify losing money on their new venture to their stockholders. After their first year, the Satellite News Channel announced it had lost $60 million. This caused their stock prices to dip and the management of both companies decided to reconsider funding the channel.

Ted seized the opportunity to bring the rivalry to an end. He offered to buy the Satellite News Channel for $25 million. ABC and Westinghouse agreed; Ted had won. Tiny Turner Broadcasting had beat two giant multinational conglomerates in a death match. The broadcasters who had written off Ted's survival chances now had to reconsider. Clearly, he was here to stay.

One casualty of the intense early years of CNN was Reese Schonfeld. Schonfeld was a professional newsman who had searched for years to find someone willing to finance a cable news channel. He had done heroic work in setting up CNN. He was also a strong willed, determined leader who demanded a great deal from his employees and did not like to have his decisions questioned. It was almost inevitable that he and Ted would conflict. Over the year 1981 and into 1982, under the intense pressure of fighting to keep the company alive, Ted and Reese began clashing, often openly and publicly. Soon it became clear that the two men could not continue working together. In May of 1982 Ted fired Schonfeld in a dispute over the hiring of conservative political commentator Pat Buchanan.

The struggle to keep CNN and Headline News alive was enough to consume all the energies of most men. Ted, however, continued to pursue other activities and business opportunities. He contracted to develop a documentary series, *Portrait of America,* with an estimated cost of $20 million. He also started Turner Educational Services, with a goal of linking television and education.

In February 1982 Ted flew to Havana, Cuba, as the guest of Fidel Castro. The Cuban dictator invited Ted because he considered CNN to be the only network that did not report the news with a bias against him. Ted toured factories, watched baseball, went to the beach and a nightclub, and duck hunted with Castro. They posed for pictures together and clowned around. They found each other very handy for favorable publicity.

"It's hard to understand how we can trade with Russia and not with him," said Ted, a self-proclaimed conservative capitalist. Many years later, this relationship proved invaluable when CNN became the first American news organization to set up a bureau in Havana.

Chapter Seven

A Better World

In July 1983, Ted took his two younger sons, Rhett and Beau, on a journey up the Amazon River with the famous explorer Captain Jacques Cousteau. They were making a documentary for the Superstation. Along the way, they endured constant rain and the sweltering heat of the dense green rain forest and viewed the animal life along the banks. Ted and Captain Cousteau also talked about the need to protect the environment.

This trip was a turning point for Ted. After the trip, he devoted a significant part of his time and fortune toward promoting the environment and peace around the world. And he made sure WTBS ran environmental documentaries by Cousteau, the Audubon Society and the National Geographic Society.

To publicize his concerns, Ted created the Better World Society to make environmental documentaries that were seen on CNN and on Chinese and Russian television. CNN, in fact, now devoted time to "positive news," including such programs as "Portrait of America," "Nice People," and "Good News." Ted pleaded for peace wherever he traveled, including the Soviet Union, although then President Reagan referred to it as the Evil Empire.

In the summer of 1984 the Soviet Union boycotted the Olympics held in Los Angeles. This was in retaliation for the U.S. boycott of the 1980 Moscow Olympics. Ted decided to hold alternative international games in 1986. He planned to call the event the Goodwill Games. He was so excited by the idea that he did somersaults down the hallway, tumbling head over heels through the executive offices.

Of course, Ted had other ideas during this period. In October 1984, he pushed a large fake button on a stage in California and began broadcasting his new Cable Music Channel. CMC was launched as an effort to stop the rapid growth of MTV. CMC went on the air the same day MTV announced the creation of its sister station, VH-1. The new station was to be aimed toward slightly older audiences than MTV. Ted's stage show attracted most of the broadcast journalists and successfully stole MTV's limelight. Its stock dropped three dollars a share.

Ted used one of the same tactics against MTV that ABC and Westinghouse had used against him in the battle between Headline News and SNC. While MTV charged cable operators a fee, Ted offered CMC free.

Many in the industry thought Ted was doing the cable

operators a favor by launching this frontal attack on MTV. They believed Ted's goal was to force the highly popular MTV to lower the rates it charged for transmitting its signal. Without competition, there was nothing to stop MTV from raising rates as much as it wanted. The speculation was that Ted wanted to help out the operators in return for their support during his battle with the networks.

Ted, however, claimed that CMC was merely part of his effort to return decency to the airwaves. MTV had created a great deal of controversy with its videos. The heavy metal videos that often used sexual and violent imagery were particularly troublesome to those who wanted to protect America's youth. "You can take a bunch of young people and you can turn them into Boy Scouts or into Hitler Youth, depending on what you teach them, and MTV's definitely a bad influence," Ted said. His intention with CMC was to change the face of music television. "I figured we'd clean it up," he said.

Ted's experiment at CMC was short-lived, however. On November 30, 1984, slightly over a month after its launching, Ted closed down CMC and, much as ABC and Westinghouse had before when it accepted defeat by CNN, sold off its assets to MTV. This time, MTV crowed about its victory. They had been in the music video business first and had fought hard to maintain its position. They announced that VH-1 would be rolled out sooner than previously planned. They also insisted

Turner's Cable Music Channel lasted only one month.

that many record companies sign exclusive deals with them. In other words, if they wanted to run their videos on MTV they could not run them on CMC. Because MTV was in many more homes than CMC, the record companies had no choice but to accept MTV's terms.

The debacle of CMC was Ted's first big embarrassment in cable broadcasting. However, there were side benefits even in this defeat. One was a strengthening of support among many conservatives who agreed that MTV was a "satanic" force in society.

Ted Turner was becoming a household name. Many in the public spoke of him admiringly. His private life, however, was not so successful. He spent little time with his family, even missing Christmas with his children on several occasions. When he was home, he ran the family as though it was an army. His son Teddy remembers, "There was a lot of yelling and tension and getting smacked around. I never could decide which was worse—having him away a lot or having him home."

Ted created a great deal of the family stress by having nearly public affairs with other women. His wife Janie often felt humiliated. Among Ted's girlfriends during these years were a former *Playboy* magazine cover girl and his personal airplane pilot.

Ted wanted his sons to endure the same hardships that Ted's father had inflicted on him. He wanted them to have the same type of military school education. He sent Teddie to McCallie, and then all three boys—Teddy, Rhett and Beau—went to the Citadel, a military college in Charleston, South Carolina.

In an effort to save their marriage, Ted and Janie began going to sessions with an Atlanta psychiatrist. The doctor diagnosed Ted as suffering from a manic-depressive disorder. This can often run in families. Manic-depressives gyrate between extreme elation and grandiosity to deep depression, despondency and guilt. Sometimes the extreme mood shifts can occur in short periods of time. The psychiatrist prescribed a drug called lithium for Ted. After taking the medication, Ted became more calm and even-tempered. The psychiatrist also determined that Ted was still troubled by the pain of his relationship with his father and needed to learn how to treat women as partners.

Another motivation for Ted to seek treatment was the acceptance that his "roller-coaster" emotional life damaged his ability to run the now giant Turner Broadcasting. Later, Ted told an interviewer how the treatment had improved his life. "I started to listen and not be judgmental and wait until someone was through rather than interrupting them, and then think about what they said before I prepared an answer. I learned to give and take better than I had previously."

By 1985, WTBS was highly profitable and CNN turned its first profit, $20 million. CNN had lost $77 million since its startup. But, five years after its beginning, Ted's gamble on twenty-four-hour news was a success. One of the secrets of his success was to plow revenues back into the company.

Ted had no intention of resting on his laurels. He started a hostile takeover bid for CBS. Ted announced in April 1985 that he would pay $5.4 billion for CBS—all in stock and bonds, no cash. Ted planned to sell off the parts of CBS—the radio stations, the record business, the book and magazine publishing. He would combine the news operations and entertainment operations of CBS and Turner Broadcasting. Ted's strategic thinking was that he needed CBS's huge audience to sell more advertising.

CBS fought Ted hard. Its management began reminding everyone of Ted's past comments and outrageous behavior.

Network officials charged the "Mouth of the South" had insulted various racial and ethnic groups. They also suggested that Turner Broadcasting was a financial house of cards and would weaken CBS. Eventually, CBS spent nearly a billion dollars to buy back much of its own stock to keep Ted from being able to purchase it. That made it impossible for Ted's plan to succeed. But even in failure, Ted won. He was now seen as a major "player" in broadcasting.

If he couldn't expand his viewership through CBS, Ted decided to expand his capacity to create programming. Ted bought the money-losing MGM movie studio for $1.5 billion. Along with the studio and production lot came 3,500 MGM films, which included 1,450 films from the old Warner Brothers and RKO studios. Included were such classics as "Gone With The Wind," "The Maltese Falcon," "The Wizard of Oz," "Citizen Kane," "Singin' In The Rain," and "It's A Wonderful Life."

There were several problems with Ted's purchase of MGM, however. While negotiating the deal with billionaire Kirk Kerkorian, a process that took over a year, several of MGM's new movie releases flopped. These losses drained more money from the corporate coffers. This decreased the value of the company and made it more difficult for Ted to arrange for loans to help pay for the stock.

The biggest problem with the MGM deal was that Ted agreed

Ted with his family in the mid-1980s. (From left) Teddy Jr., Laura, Jennie, Ted, Janie, Rhett, Beau.

to pay far too much for control of the film company. Most analysts agreed that $1.5 billion was at least $200 million more than its true value. This was typical of Ted. He was convinced that buying MGM was the right thing to do to ensure the long-term growth of his company.

In the end, the purchase was only made possible by the use of so-called "junk bonds." Michael Milliken, who later went to prison for breaking many of the laws that govern corporate transactions, was instrumental in arranging for the marketing of the bonds. At the conclusion of the deal, Ted was in debt for over $2 billion dollars. Shortly after closing the deal, Ted realized that his control of Turner Broadcasting was at risk.

Ted had risked his company several times before. This time was different, though. The MGM deal was structured so that every month that passed without him being able to make a payment on the huge debt automatically turned over a chunk of Turner Broadcasting stock to Kerkorian. With each passing month his control of the company he built was being handed over to someone else.

The pressure began getting to Ted. One night he was having dinner with his mother and some friends at his plantation Kinlock, located in the South Carolina low country. Instead of eating, Ted began pacing the dining room. Suddenly he shouted out "I've really done it this time."

Ted's mother tried to assure him. She reminded him that he

had been in tough situations before and had always come through.

"How the hell am I going to pay that two billion dollars?" he asked.

His mother's face turned white. "Did you say two billion dollars?" she asked.

"Sure," Ted said. "I told you it was gonna cost two billion dollars to get MGM."

"Oh my," she said. "I thought you said two million."

One of Ted's oldest dreams had been to own a movie studio. He idolized Jack Warner, Louis B. Mayer, and the other past masters of Hollywood. Owning a studio was the crown jewel of the purchase of MGM. But making movies is highly expensive and risky. Because of the debt he acquired in buying MGM, there was simply no money to risk in a studio. Ted realized he would have to sell everything but the film library.

Because he was strapped for cash, Ted took a major loss when he sold the studio. His impulsiveness had lost him millions. He was in real danger of losing everything he had worked his entire life to build.

The threat of bankruptcy eventually led to a deal with Ted's customers in the cable industry. A group that included cable system owners and others agreed to buy thirty-seven percent of TBS stock. They also insisted on the right to block any big purchases of the sort that had gotten him into such deep financial trouble. Ted had lost control of his company. Under this new arrangement, there were regular conflicts between his seat-of-the-pants style and ecological concerns and his partners' focus on making steady profits.

In the midst of this turmoil, Ted still found time to attend the July 1986 Goodwill Games in Moscow. Thirty-five hundred Eastern Bloc and Western athletes competed in everything from track and field to tennis, from judo to yachting. During the games he spoke with Soviet leader Mikhail Gorbachev about the need for cooperation to prevent nuclear war. Each day of the games, from early morning to midnight, he was a bundle of energy as he handed out medals, gave speeches, and hosted receptions.

Unfortunately, few spectators or participants came to the games. Several champion athletes stayed away for fear of radiation from the nuclear meltdown at Chernobyl that had occurred in 1986. Few watched the games at home. TBS lost $20 million in advertising. But Ted thought he was doing great things for world peace.

Janie finally tired of being Ted's neglected wife. They divorced in 1987. For a while, Ted lived with one of the girlfriends. They bought a rustic lodge on the California coast together and enjoyed the outdoor life. He, however, was determined not to marry again so soon.

In 1987 Ted received bad publicity for colorizing classic

movies such as *The Maltese Falcon* and *It's a Wonderful Life* from the MGM collection. Among those speaking out against Ted were the legendary movie director John Huston, who had directed *The Maltese Falcon*, actor Jimmy Stewart, who had starred in *It's a Wonderful Life*, and contemporary moviemakers such as Woody Allen and Martin Scorcese.

Ted saw colorizing as a sound business decision. It should raise the market value of his movie library because the audiences for color movies were much larger than the ones for black and white. And, as he said, "Anybody who really wants to see the movies in black and white can buy a videocassette of the film. They're all available."

The Atlanta Braves contributed to making 1987 a bad year for Ted by losing their first eight games at home.

But CNN, at least, continued to have successes—for its coverage of an earthquake in Mexico City, the hijacking of a TWA plane in the Middle East, and the explosion of space shuttle Challenger as it tried to carry seven astronauts into orbit.

After the setbacks of 1987, and the restrictions placed on him by the new board of directors for TBS, Ted hunkered down the next few years and concentrated on turning his company around. There were no more flashy hostile takeover attempts, or financially draining efforts to promote world peace. The medication he was taking for his manic-depression also enabled him to stay centered on his job.

By 1989, Ted's newest cable channel, TNT, was attracting large audiences by showing the old movies purchased from MGM. The MGM deal, with its syndication and programming possibilities, was now beginning to pay off. TNT also showed original dramatic and sports productions, including professional football. His old standby, "Superstation" WTBS, was now the single most watched basic cable channel in the country, and his networks were earning more than ABC and CBS combined.

The success of TNT (and later TCM—Turner Classic Movies) proved that Ted's initial vision when he purchased the MGM film library had been sound. The rapid expansion of networks soon made Turner Broadcasting the most prominent cable program provider in the world.

An ironic result of the MGM acqusition was that in 1992 the MGM Board of Directors, who had made no effort to hide that they thought they had taken advantage of Ted in the original deal, sued Turner Broadcasting. Their argument was that Ted had paid too little for the film library. They claimed that Ted had hidden the real value of the movies in his negotiations. The lawsuit was later dropped.

CNN and its companion Headline News reached nearly fifty-one million homes in the U.S. and eighty-three nations abroad. The once poor CNN made profits of $85 million a year, had 4,000 part-time and 1,600 full-time employees in twenty-one bureaus around the world. Margaret Thatcher, Francois

Mitterand, Mikhail Gorbachev and Fidel Castro all watched CNN faithfully in their offices. Saudi Arabia's King Fahd was said to watch compulsively all through the night. Even North Korea's supposedly isolated dictator Kim Il Sung was a "subscriber."

CNN reported from the scene of big events, such as the San Francisco earthquake and the fall of the Berlin Wall, which signaled the beginning of the end for the Soviet Empire. In June 1989, CNN was at Tiananmen Square in Beijing, when the autocratic Chinese government rolled tanks over demonstrating students. CNN broadcast its own reporters being thrown off the air after the troops invaded the square.

Ted was especially proud of the "internationalism" of his network. He started a regular show on CNN called "World Report." "As an American, I always thought of the world as 'President Reagan talked to [British Prime Minister] Margaret Thatcher' or 'President Bush talks to Gorbachev,'" he said. "But on World Report you'll see the president of an African country meeting with another African leader. And that never makes the news here."

By 1990, viewers on six continents watched CNN. It was inevitable that the success of twenty-four-hour news would attract competition. Rupert Murdoch, who has emerged as Ted's biggest broadcasting opponent, started Sky News in Europe as direct competition.

Ted often expressed the wish that he could show his father his vast empire. His father's legacy hung on in other ways. When he turned fifty, Ted admitted he had not expected to live that long. He expected an assassin or suicide to end his life. He knew that he wanted to spend more time in the outdoors. In typical Ted fashion, on a visit to a friend in Wyoming, he bought a ranch sight unseen through a broker who sent him brochures. The Bar None ranch spread out over 20,000 acres.

Ted also traveled to China in 1990. He climbed the Great Wall and toured the Forbidden City—the old imperial compound in the center of Beijing. He visited the Chinese prime minister. He toured the Middle East and lectured Israelis and Arabs on the need for peace in the region. He went swimming in the Dead Sea with King Hussein of Jordan and talked about Middle East politics with Palestinian leader Yassir Arafat.

Ted enjoyed his Montana ranch so much he decided to buy a second. The Flying D had 130,000 acres and a fully functioning cattle operation. Ted loved to roam his ranches. His love of wildlife and of the land was evident to anyone who walked the wide-open spaces with him.

Chapter Eight

New Directions

Ted met the actress and exercise video producer Jane Fonda in the summer of 1989 at a Los Angeles fundraiser. Ted asked her for a date, but she had recently gone through a bitter divorce and rebuffed him.

By 1990, however, they began dating steadily. Jane accompanied him when he dined with President Bush at the White House, with Soviet President Gorbachev at the Kremlin, and with French President Mitterand at the Elysee Palace in Paris.

Jane took Ted to the Academy Award presentation for that year. Ted, who claimed to be a movie lover, did not know she had won two best-actress Oscars. One had been for *Klute* in 1971 and the other for *Coming Home* in 1978. Jane also convinced him to take up regular exercising. He lost eighteen pounds.

Ted invited Jane and her brother, the actor Peter Fonda, to his new ranch. He took her everywhere on a whirlwind courtship, showing her off to stunned CNN employees in New York.

Ted was chivalrous in her presence, and Jane soon realized he was comfortable around a strong woman.

Ted and Jane's relationship became the talk of the entertainment and business worlds. Jane was a controversial political activist who had gone to Vietnam to protest America's war with that country. Ted was a Southern conservative. As one observer noted, "It was hard to imagine a spectrum they wouldn't be at opposite ends of: She wanted to liberate the world; he wanted to own it. She was politically correct before the term was coined; he was an equal-opportunity offender—blacks, Jews, Italians, the handicapped, everyone. She was Hollywood royalty; he was the evil captain of colorization. She was a passionate feminist; and he was, as he announced on one of their first dates, 'a male chauvinist pig.'"

The couple did have some things in common. Of course, their money, fame, age and reputations for impulsive love affairs were well known. But, maybe most importantly, each was shadowed by the suicide of a parent. Jane's mother had killed herself when she was a child. They also shared total commitment to a clean environment. Ted and Jane launched a "Save the Earth" campaign in New York and attended the Earth Summit in Rio de Janeiro, the capital of Brazil. They held talks on the fate of the Mayan Indians at Harvard University.

When they weren't giving speeches, they were at his ranch, one of the eleven homes he now owned around the country. Ted shocked his cattle-rancher neighbors by announcing he would be returning the land to its natural state. From now on, wildlife would roam freely, and buffalo would be raised for sale. Ted and Jane liked to watch the wildlife through telescopes. They liked to ride or walk around his 130,000 Montana acres looking for Indian arrowheads or trout fishing. Sometimes, former president Carter joined them.

By November of 1990 Ted and Jane were engaged to be married.

After CNN's 1991 triumph in covering the Persian Gulf War, the upstart channel that had once been derided as the "Chicken Noodle Network," now occupied center stage in world news coverage. Seventy-five million people around the world watched the war on CNN. Even President George Bush would later acknowledge that he learned more from CNN than from his spy agencies.

CNN had also become a major player in world diplomacy. It was the one network that all world leaders regularly turned to for news of the war. CNN even played a role in ending the Gulf War by interviewing world leaders while other leaders watched them on TV. First, one leader would propose an idea, then he would watch the reaction on CNN from the others, and then he would revise his proposal.

When Russian leader Boris Yeltsin climbed on a tank to halt the attempted 1991 Soviet coup, he knew his image would be flashed by CNN to hundreds of thousands of Muscovites, letting them know that he was still in control.

In October of 1991, Ted's Atlanta Braves made it to the World Series, though they lost in seven games to the Minnesota Twins. During one of the games, the nationwide television broadcast showed Ted sound asleep on Jane's shoulder as one of his Braves rounded the bases after hitting a grand slam home run. This was clearly a different Ted Turner than the wild man who had pushed a ball around the infield with his nose.

Ted and Jane were married that December at his Florida estate outside Tallahassee. His marriage to Jane Fonda symbolized how much Ted had changed. "I was raised to be a political conservative, but I've become more of a progressive over the last fifteen years," he explained at the time. "I've gone from rampant nationalist to rampant internationalist. I've gone from someone in the billboard business to someone in the television business, from someone who was racing sailboats to fly-fishing. From male chauvinist to being totally in favor of the equal sharing of power and responsibility—men and women. I'm going to be a totally different kind of husband this time."

His son Teddy finally thought of his father as someone he could have fun with—and credited the change to Jane. Under her influence, Ted had become openly affectionate with his own children and even checked in regularly with Jane's two children.

During the early 1990s, Ted Tuner's media empire grew

Ted and Jane Fonda's wedding, December 21, 1991.

Ted and Jane met with Soviet leader Gorbachev in 1990.

even larger. In December of 1991, he bought Hanna-Barbera Productions, producer of "The Flintstones", "Yogi Bear" and "Huckleberry Hound" cartoons. That gave him control of 3,000 half hours of animation. Ted used this programming to start the Cartoon Network.

Ted also rented his new treasure trove of cartoons to the other networks. This had become his standard practice since buying MGM. He reused all his resources to maximize the value. As one observer noted, he might show "the same John Wayne movies on TBS and TNT," then sell them as videos "and again to local stations."

Ted wears a cartoon tie as he announces the launching of the Cartoon Network in 1992.

Meanwhile, Turner Broadcasting, his umbrella company, had become the largest news gathering agency in the world. Said one observer: "CNN distributes live news packages to more than six hundred television stations worldwide. CNN's audio track provides core programming for CNN Radio, which is distributed to several hundred independent and government-owned broadcasters around the world. Turner has extended his reach into the U.S. educational market with a satellite-delivered news package, replete with printed classroom materials, which goes into nearly twenty thousand secondary and high schools across the country. CNN produces a highly regarded opinion poll in conjunction with *Time* magazine and also co-produces entertainment industry news programming with *Variety.* CNN coverage of world crises like the Gulf War and the collapse of Soviet communism also gets repackaged into books published by Turner Publishing. Turner Home Entertainment takes CNN news footage, TNT movies, and cartoon channel animation and repackages the lot for sale in videocassette format."

Turner Broadcasting also began making films for his cable television channel TNT. He also became personally involved in the making of the civil war feature movie *Gettysburg.* Ted realized a lifelong fantasy by playing a bit part as a dying Confederate officer in the movie. To further expand his reach, Ted launched the first commercial television station in Russia in 1993.

Ted and Gerald Levin announce the merger of Turner Broadcasting and Time-Warner Communications, September 22, 1995.

Ted was always thinking of new ways to expand either his distribution or his program access. In pursuit of this goal, he began talking to networks and studios about a merger, a buyout, or a partnership. He even tried another merger with CBS.

Then, in 1996, Ted stunned the media world again by merging Turner Broadcasting with Time-Warner. This merger matched a pattern in the industry. Disney had bought ABC, and Westinghouse was about to buy CBS. To both Ted Turner and Time-Warner, it made sense for them to combine forces.

The merger was a shrewd business move for all concerned. But the deal ended Ted Turner's career as an independent businessman. For thirty-four years he had headed a company with his name on it. Now he was part of the Time Warner management team, with the title of vice president in charge of Turner Broadcasting. The big question was whether Ted could subordinate his ego and work for another corporation. Other flamboyant entrepreneurs, such as Ross Perot, had not been able to make the transition from chief boss to one among equals.

On a personal level, Ted finally seemed to be in control of his impulses. By 1995, he had stopped taking lithium.

There are plenty of challenges in the communications industry. Even before the merger with Time-Warner, Microsoft, the giant computer software company founded by Bill Gates, joined with NBC to form MSNBC, an around-the-clock news channel. And Ted's nemesis, Rupert Murdoch, launched the Fox News Channel.

Ted enjoying himself at the dinner held after his announcement of a gift of one billion dollars to the United Nations, September 18, 1997.

Ted's involvement in Turner Broadcasting continues. Early in 1997 his long relationship with Cuban dictator Fidel Castro finally paid off. CNN was the first organization to open a news bureau in Havana after the U.S. government allowed it. Ted also announced a new service, called CNN Custom News. It offered consumers free personalized news over the World Wide Web. Computer users could design personal web pages that reflect their interests by drawing information from CNN.

In September 1996, Ted and Jane bought their largest ranch yet, the 578,000-acre Vermejo Park Ranch in the Sangre de Cristo Mountains of northeastern New Mexico. One of the legendary saloons of the Old West, the St. James, is located on the ranch's property. Its tin ceiling is pocked with thumb-sized holes from century-old gunfights and the old guest book includes the names of Annie Oakley, Jesse James and Buffalo Bill Cody.

Ted now owned three ranches in New Mexico and five in Montana and Wyoming. Vermejo Park reportedly cost $100 million. Covering 903 square miles and stretching into four counties of New Mexico and Colorado, the ranch is only slightly smaller than the state of Rhode Island. Ted now owns more land than any other American. Here, as in Montana, Ted replaced the existing cattle with 4,000 buffalo.

As new residents of New Mexico, Ted and Jane have donated millions of dollars from their Turner Foundation to thirty-three local environmental groups. The foundation's board—Ted is the president—consists of Jane and Ted's children. Their goals are to support preservation of the environment, natural resources and wildlife, and to work on population issues in the United States and abroad. They hope it will soon become the largest environmental foundation in the United States with more than $1 billion in its treasury.

In September 1997, Ted stunned the world, as he has done so many times before, when he announced that he would make a gift of $1 billion to the United Nations. The gift will be spread over ten years. Ted wants the money to be spent on United Nations humanitarian projects for children, the environment, refugees, landmine clearance and other efforts to help poor people. In presenting the gift, Ted challenged other American billionaires to help out in the same way.

Today, Ted and Jane focus much of their time on the environment and humanitarian efforts. He is still involved in running Turner Broadcasting, however. In this capacity he angered many in the motion picture industry by refusing to air a movie that was contracted for TNT. The film, *Bastard Out of Carolina*, was a stark look at sexual and physical child abuse. The movie's director, Anjelica Huston, argued publicly that Ted was using his immense wealth and power to censor her moviemaking. Ted simply said he thought the movie was unsuitable for television and refused to run it on TNT.

Although his face is craggy and his hair silvery-white, Ted Turner continues to play a role in many of the critical issues of today. As a senior executive with Time Warner, he will have an influence on the future of the telecommunications and entertainment industries. But his main concern now is to help stop the physical destruction of the Earth, and to help make safe places for the world's people to live. These are huge tasks, but if Ted Turner's past is any guide, he might succeed at a level few today think possible.

Time-Warner's Holdings

(Ted owns 10% of Time-Warner's stock)

TIME WARNER PUBLISHING
WARNER BOOKS
Warner Treasurers
Warner Vision
Aspect
LITTLE, BROWN
Bullfinch
Back Bay
MAIL-ORDER BOOKS
Time-Life Books
Oxmoor House
Book-of-the-Month Club
Sunset Books

MOTION PICTURES
Warner Brothers (75%)
Castle Rock Entertainment
New Line Cinema
Library of MGM, RKO and
pre-1950 Warner Brothers films

CABLE & SATELLITE TV
CNN
Headline News
CNNfn
CNN Airport Network
CNN Interactive
CNN/SI
CNN Newsource
TBS Superstation
Cinemax
Comedy Central (50%)
Court TV (33.3%)
Sega Channel (33%)
Turner Classic Movies
TNT
Cartoon Network
HBO (75%)
Primestar (31%)

CABLE FRANCHISES
12.1 million subscribers (about 20% of U.S. TV homes)

TV PROGRAMMING
Warner Brothers Television
WB Television Network (with Chicago Tribune)
Warner Brothers Television Animation (75%)
Warner Brothers International Television (75%)
Telepictures Production
Hanna-Barbera Cartoons

World Championship Wrestling
Turner Original Productions
Turner Sports
Turner Learning (noncom-
mercial daily newscasts for
schools)

MUSIC
Atlantic Elektra Warner labels
(22% of U.S. music sales)

RADIO
CNNRadio

MAGAZINES
Asiaweek
People Weekly
Baby Talk
People en Espaol
Coastal Living
Cooking Light
President
Dancyu
Progressive Farmer
DC Comics
Entertainment
Southern Living Weekly
Southern Accents
Fortune
Health
Sports Illustrated
Hippocrates
In Style
Sports Illustrated for Kids
Life
Money
Parenting

Sunset
This Old House
Time
Time for Kids
Weight Watchers
Who

THEME PARKS:
Six Flags (49%)

SPORTS
Atlanta Braves
Atlanta Hawks
Goodwill Games

MISCELLANEOUS
Home video and
satellite, CD-ROM
production, some retail stores

Timeline

1938 Ted born to Robert Edward and Florence Turner in Cincinnati, Ohio.

1947: Sent to Georgia Military Academy in Atlanta.

1950: Sent to McCallie Military Academy, Chattanooga, Tennessee.

1956: Starts Brown University, Providence, Rhode Island.

1960: Marries Judy Nye in Chicago. Ted's sister, Mary Jean, dies of encephalitis brought on by lupus.

1961: Daughter Laura Lee born.

1962: Ted divorces Judy.

1963: Judy returns; suicide of Ed Turner. Ted buys outdoor advertising companies back from Naegele; birth of Robert Edward (Teddy)IV.

1964: Marries Jane Smith.

1967: Sails across Atlantic to Copenhagen.

1969: Competes in World Ocean Racing Championship.

1970: Named Yachtsman of the Year; buys WTCG (later WTBS).

1973: Named Yachtsman of the Year for a second time; admitted to New York Yacht Club. Begins showing Atlanta Braves games on WTBS.

1974: Competes in America's Cup.

1976: WTBS distributed by satellite throughout North America. Ted buys the Atlanta Braves.

1977: Suspended by the Commissioner of Baseball. Wins America's Cup. Named Yachtsman of the Year for a third time.

1979: Survives massive storm to win Fastnet race off English coast.

1980: CNN begins broadcasting. Ted competes in America's Cup for third time.

1982: Headline News begins broadcasting.

1985: Ted attempts takeover of CBS; buys MGM's film library.

1986: Attends first Goodwill Games in Moscow.

1987: Divorces Janie.

1988: TNT starts broadcasting.

1989: Ted buys first western ranch—the Bar None in Wyoming; begins courting Jane Fonda.

1990: Buys second ranch, the Flying D, in Montana.

1991: CNN scoops the world with its live Gulf War coverage from Baghdad. CNN helps Boris Yeltsin block a coup by the enemies of Russian democracy. The Braves play in the World Series against the Minnesota Twins. Ted buys the animation studio Hanna-Barbera. Ted and Jane are married

1996: Turner Communications merges with Time-Warner.

1997: CNN opens bureau in Cuba. Ted donates $1 billion to the United Nations.

Bibliography

Advertising Age, 15 January 1996.

Bibb, Porter. *It Ain't As Easy As It Looks*. New York, Crown Publishers, Inc., 1993.

Business Week, 18 October 1993.

Electronic Media, 21 May 1990.

Esquire, November, 1995.

Goldberg, Robert and Gerald Jay Goldberg. *Citizen Turner*. New York: Harcourt, Brace and Co., 1995.

Good Housekeeping, February, 1996.

New Woman, December, 1993.

Time, 6 January 1992.

U.S. News & World Report, 10 April 1995.

Vaughan, Roger. *The Grand Gesture*. Boston: Little-Brown and Company, 1975.

Vaughan, Roger. *Ted Turner: The Man Behind The Mouth*. Boston: Sail Books, Inc., 1978.

Whittemore, Hank. *CNN: The Inside Story*. Boston: Little Brown and Company, 1990.

Williams, Christian. *Lead, Follow or Get Out Of The Way: The Story of Ted Turner*. New York: Times Books, 1981.

Index